TRIALS AND **TRIP**ULATIONS

Observances by a North Carolina Attorney
with an Intra-state Practice

Robert M. Weinstein, Esq.

authorHOUSE®

AuthorHouse™
1663 Liberty Drive
Bloomington, IN 47403
www.authorhouse.com
Phone: 1 (800) 839-8640

Published by AuthorHouse 07/27/2017

ISBN: 978-1-5246-9092-2 (sc)
ISBN: 978-1-5246-9091-5 (e)

Library of Congress Control Number: 2017906952

CONTENTS

DEDICATION

This book of observations is dedicated to the court personnel in the many counties visited who exhibited warmth and kindness when asked for information and/or directions. A stranger was welcomed time and time again. This represents another element of the beauty of North Carolina.

PREFACE

This tutorial was created for the benefit of North Carolina attorneys as they represent their clients in different courthouses in our beautiful State. It is hoped that the observances noted will make for more confident travels, which could prove to be educational as well. Many sights and sounds await the traveler, be it on a crowded expressway or on a quaint country road. This is all in pursuit of the objective of being present on behalf of your client at the call of the calendar where ever that might be. Once trips have been made to other counties, and "you have learned your way around", subsequent journeys will be made with much more ease. Any possible delays should always be factored into your anticipated departure time and the important arrival time, all subject to existing highway and weather conditions. It is hoped that the beauty of North Carolina will be embraced and that a few minutes can be taken from time to time to learn of the significant historical aspects of each county seat visited. Often, an early departure will be required. Hopefully, the observances mentioned in this tutorial will ease the stress of a lengthy trip. When you visit another County's Courthouse, you may feel you are out of your comfort zone. You will find new surroundings and new faces, all meshed together by the North Carolina Court System and its state-wide Rules of Civil Procedure. If you travel to the same counties often, you will become acquainted with the personnel in the Clerk's Offices as well as the Courtrooms. This frequency will also enable you to easily engineer your path to the Courthouse, to available parking facilities and to the necessary courtrooms. It is a privilege to practice law in the State of North Carolina and to represent clients in such beautiful surroundings. This beauty is magnified by the visits from time to time and to place to place. This tutorial is for the attorney "road warriors' who travel on North Carolina highways and roads, and to those who await their safe return back in the office and at home.

Robert M. Weinstein, Esq.

THE JOURNEY

You are handling a matter that needs to be heard in the county where suit was filed. You have checked a map to determine the approximate distance you will need to travel the morning of the hearing. You are now able to obtain directions to the courthouse from the web-site of the North Carolina Administration of the Courts. You are also blessed by the wonderful highway systems here in North Carolina. The Interstate Highway System is at your service between the larger towns and cities. At this time, I-40 handles the east and west destinations, and I-85 and I-95 are for your north and south travels. The North Carolina State Roads will enable you to reach courthouses in rural, less populated areas. Some trips may require the utilization of both the Interstate Systems and State Roads depending on the location of your destination. President Dwight D. Eisenhower was the moving force behind the wonderful Interstate Highway System and Governor W. Kerr Scott made sure most of rural state roads in North Carolina were paved. You have each to thank as you make your way through our beautiful State. North Carolina has the largest state-maintained highway system in the U.S., with 77,400 miles of roads.

The time of year of your trip to your hearing will dictate how long you should anticipate the trip to take to achieve your goals of: (1) finding the courthouse, (2) finding a place to park, and (3) finding your courtroom, all before the call of the calendar. During the winter months, you need to factor in possibly becoming involved with sleet, ice and snow along the way. If snow is already on the ground, the Interstate System is usually kept clear by heavy truck traffic. The same cannot be said for the rural roads which could become treacherous. Additional time for travel should be allotted if such be the case. No matter the time of year, always plan your trip with the idea that *there will be* some delay either by an accident, heavy traffic, or highway construction. Your file should reflect the telephone number of the clerk's office or the court administrator's office so they can be called from your cell phone should you find that you will be delayed. A quick message to the courtroom clerk regarding the anticipated delay will then be possible.

In North Carolina, all seasons are beautiful times of year to travel to court in other counties. In the winter, the beauty of a shiny field of frozen dew is spectacular. The spring brings new growth and a general 'greening' all around. In the summer, you can expect fields of corn, cotton and soybeans as well as stunning sunflower beds for as far as the eye can see. The fall, of course, produces the magnificent changes of color to bright reds and yellow, and all colors in between. It is from State Roads that you observe these seasonal changes, up close and personal. The citizens who live on these roads take pride in their lawns. They are all perfectly manicured.

As you travel on State Roads, you will find that private flower gardens add to the beauty of the scenery as you past houses, farms and fields. In these personal gardens, an assortment of flowers grow as well as produce for family consumption such as corn, cucumbers and squash. The many garages and barns protect all vehicles, pick-up trucks, tractors as well as bales of hay. There is often an ample supply of rusting automobiles and equipment tucked to the side of the property and placed in a fashion that they would be inconspicuous.

While enjoying these ever changing sites of color and contrast, and if your journey to court consumes an hour or perhaps several hours, you will be using your radio or disc player. Today, there several excellent news and sports shows all during the day to keep you abreast of highlights, predictions, and in depth analysis. In the alternative, you may have recorded on a CD facts regarding your case, the issues, your proposed argument and as well as an outline of your question pattern. This could be very positive in supporting your confidence and familiarity of the facts.

You should take advantage of the quiet in your vehicle. There are no interruptions without your consent. Another factor which needs to be considered is the type of music you may be listening to after you have reviewed your facts. as the case may be. Music can have a profound influence on your state of mind, often in a positive sense but also in a negative sense. Country songs about heartbreak, trains and hitch-hiking in the rain are to be avoided. Such can produce a mood not conducive to formulating and supporting a legal argument in Court on behalf of your client. If you need to be surrounded by music during your trip, melodies without words would be your best bet, such as classical compositions. Quiet, soothing tunes are a must to promote a good 'frame of mind' to perform successfully. Music and mood are closely interrelated. It has been shown that a positive mood allows the human brain to think more creatively. This will hold you in good stead during case presentation and argument. It will boost your confidence as well.

If you are travelling on an Interstate Highway, you can expect to find county supported Rest Stops at designated intervals with signage providing advance notification of same. Most stops are very clean and some provide information to the traveler of present locations with a large wall map. Local businesses often provide advertising in neatly stacked hand-outs. Once you learn of the location of the rest stops, your travels on interstate highways to Courts in neighboring counties become more confident. The same 'stretch of interstate' will carry you to a number of county seats.

While travelling on State Roads, your rest stop will be at small 'quick-stop' gasoline stations/curb markets. Most proprietors are knowledgeable should you need directions. In exchange for the rest and information, the purchase of some gasoline, a soft drink and a snack is made possible. Many such stops in smaller communities are in the fashion of a country store with a variety of staples, meat products and produce. There are always appropriate facilities for the you, the traveler. If you do not need to stop on the way to Court, you have locked in on a future stop on the way back to your office or perhaps the next time you are in the area.

PARKING DURING COURT VISIT

Once the courthouse has been found, you need to find a parking place for your car. Parking facilities will vary from county to county, and will depend on the size of the population who will be using the facilities at any one time. In metropolitan areas, you will find a number of 'parking decks'. You can anticipate walking one to three blocks from the 'parking deck' to the courthouse so this additional time should be factored in the time you have allotted for yourself to be present for the Call of the Calendar. Once in the courthouse itself, you will need to navigate the elevators and to find your courtroom once on the proper floor. However, before you leave your 'parking deck', make sure you have noted the floor number and color as well as the number of your space.

After coming off the highway and finding your way to park your car, there is a tendency to rush off, if in fact you were delayed on your way. Many decks are side by side. Take the time, also, to note the address of your deck - street name and number. These few steps will save lots of time once you are ready to find your car and to travel back to your office. Some decks have multiple inverted floors, some heading up and the others down. You will enter the deck early in the day with many spots available. When you return, the decks will be packed so any preliminary steps taken as mentioned above will come in handy. The ticket-takers at these decks are usually cordial and are willing to assist you in navigating, perhaps, one-way streets as you work your way back to the highway "on your way back home". Once you have visited this particular county several times, you will know your way around the streets and the available parking facilities.

In medium sized counties, you will find an assortment of smaller 'parking decks' and parking lots. Some lots are reserved for court personnel only. Wherever you park, pay close attention to area, the adjoining street, etc. so there will be no problems or delay in locating your vehicle. Metered parking spaces will also be available. Factor in the time allotted by the meter with the time you anticipate being needed that morning in Court. Going out to "feed the meter" can be a hassle. A parking ticket is the essence of aggravation so you will have to 'choose your poison' as you decide where to leave your vehicle. A parking deck or a parking lot with an attendant may be your best bet if there is a chance that your Hearing or Trial could be protracted.

Smaller counties present more casual modes of parking. There are paved and unpaved lots. Parking on the streets is also an option. Often, there are no meters. There is usually a sign declaring a two hour maximum at some parking lots and parking spaces.

THE COURTHOUSE

The county courthouse records the life and times of its citizens. Births, marriages, divorces, deaths, real estate transactions and all happenings in between including but not limited to suits, judgments, foreclosures and claims of lien. It is the public record keeper for and of the citizens. Initially, courthouses were located in or near the center of the county seat to provide easy access to the citizens. They were located on prominent thorough-fares and often in circles in the middle of town.

As you journey toward the courthouse, you will note that older houses and small buildings have been converted to Law Offices. The closer you get to the courthouse itself, the more prevalent is this type of Law Office. The physical address of the Courthouse may or may not assist you. Courthouse Square or Circle are helpful as is Main Street,

Governmental Plaza and Governmental Center. Once the courthouse is found the first time, future visits are more leisurely. During the early days, very few courthouses had security equipment in place at the entrances. But now, the security lines at the entrances can be quite long so this further delay should be factored into your court appearance time-table. Each county issues to its attorneys badges which entitles entry without having the go through the security process. Always take your home badge with you as some counties will honor your home badge once they have established the fact that you are an attorney. In some counties, you can avoid the delay of the security process by exhibiting your North Carolina State Bar identification card Once these initial steps are completed, you can then seek your courtroom. You can advise a Deputy Sheriff the nature of your case. He or she can advise you as correct courtroom. At times, the courtroom number will differ from the printed information if the calendar becomes populated with more cases. You are now ready for the calendar call. More times than not, Court is opened on time which is always appreciated in view of the time and effort invested to be present on time on behalf of your client.

As the population grew, more services were required causing the courthouses to build annexes. When you visited these courthouses, and as you walked down the hallways, you could note the changes in the flooring from black and white tile, solid color and then, in some instances, to linoleum. This denotes physical "stretch-marks" as there are expansions through the years to meet the growing needs of its citizenry. In time, the courthouse property will reach a saturation point forcing the courthouses to relocate to larger tracts of land to accommodate the services now required by the increased county population. The older structures would remain intact. Thereafter, it would be known as "the old courthouse" and would be utilized with offices for, perhaps, the board of elections, a county museum or meeting place for local women's clubs. It remained a solid structure in a prominent location. Often, the exterior received a 'face-lift' and continued to be a focal point in the town although not as the courthouse.

During holiday seasons, this structure would be beautifully decorated. Its grounds would remain manicured and its flowering shrubbery pruned. It would remain "the old courthouse" on town maps and on any historical signage. The new courthouse is often located a mile or so from the center of town, usually in a area heavy with trees and new landscapes. There is now a special parking area near the entrance. New courthouses have a somewhat 'modern' feel, with more glass than before and more sharp angles for the walls and roofline. This newness is reflected by smaller courtrooms. In the older courthouses, the courtrooms were very spacious, with portraits of former Judges, many of whom are now deceased. In some counties, the new courthouse is built right next to the old one, with the older structure becoming 'an annex' for use by the county government. The parking area is then expanded to accommodate the needs of the court employees as well as the visitors to both the new courthouse and 'the annex'. Many of the older courthouses contain information as to present and past county commissioners, the dates they served and, often, their pictures. The history of the county itself is often displayed pictorially. Veterans of some or all wars are honored either in the courthouse itself or on its front lawn as the case may be.

Many counties have elaborate monuments to honor all who have served, especially those who paid the ultimate price to protect our freedoms. The smaller counties have larger areas in front of the courthouse to display these memorials of recognition and of the appreciation of the citizenry for the bravery of those who served. Tall marble tributes can often be found as well as actual bells and cannons from battles past. In larger counties where land in and around the courthouse is somewhat limited, recognition of the service and sacrifice of its veterans is often in the form of plaques on the front wall of the courthouse, inside and out. Newer courthouses use marble fronts in which to etch passages which reflect the pursuit of justice as well as to honor veterans from all wars for their service and sacrifice.

In the newer structures, an extra floor or two, initially empty, are incorporated for future expansion. In addition, the newer courthouses are more 'customer friendly' than their predecessors in the sense of 'finding your way around' with more ease and less confusion. The elevator banks are now located in such a way so as to enable a free flow of traffic to the courtrooms, etc. New attorneys will benefit from this improvement, also. Local attorneys are acquainted with all facets of the new courthouse. It is the attorney from another county, coming to this county for the first time, who will greatly appreciate this new convenience, after the courthouse was located and suitable parking secured.

COURTHOUSE SECURITY

When you enter a courthouse in North Carolina, you will note in most counties that security measures are in place. In such a case, the visitor will approach a screening station where he/she will be required empty pockets, and to surrender wallets, watches, belts, etc and to walk through some form of metal detection equipment. Any briefcases, pocketbooks, etc. are placed on the security screening conveyor belt. These steps are taken to ensure that court patrons are not carrying any weapons or contraband on their persons that can be perceived as a weapon. Any weapons or contraband that are located on an individual will be seized and the subject will face possible legal action. Effective February 3, 2014, a ban on cell phones and other electronic devices at the Guilford County Courthouse also went into effect. In addition to cell phones, the ban concerns cameras, computers, electronic tablets and other electronic communication devices. The courthouse ban now also includes cell phone chargers, Bluetooth headsets, ear buds, and other select electronic devices. The rationale is that if no communication or electronic devices are allowed within the courthouse without a permit, then there is no need for accessories. Court officials said cell phones, in and of themselves, were disruptive to court proceedings and have become too much of a nuisance. Also, there are safety concerns after someone was recently caught taking pictures of witnesses, jurors, judges or others during court proceedings. Another contributing instance was when persons began sitting on the floors in the hallways, taking pictures and texting inside courtrooms, playing video games and music, with there being shouts at people over phones and tablets.

In the state of North Carolina as far as courthouses are concerned, there is the following arrangement: the Judges and Court Administrators are state employees **controlling the operation** of the courts and promulgating the rules, with the county **owning** the building(s) and being responsible for cleaning the maintaining the facilities. The county also provides security in the courthouse as well as on its perimeter and at the entrances. Those entering the courthouse will be informed of this ban before going through the required 'metal detector'. One time, Davidson County Sheriff's Deputies arrested a man carrying a weapon into the county courthouse. He walked to a security check-point, putting his coat on the table. He then walked through the scanner. A deputy put the man's coat in a scanner and discovered a weapon described as being a .380 caliber handgun. He faces charges of possession of a weapon on state property or a courthouse and carrying a concealed weapon. He was placed in the county jail on $6,500.00 bail. What was the man's mindset? Who were the intended victims? An ex-spouse, the prosecutor, the Judge? It is frightening just to think about it. It is also frightening to realize that not so long ago, many counties did not have a 'security check point' upon entering the courthouse. At the entrance of the Guilford County Courthouse, the county has installed small storage boxes which can be rented for 25 cents. The boxes will open with a key. Attorneys, paralegals, court personnel and others who have received special pass from the county will be exempt from the above-mentioned security procedure.

The writer, as an attorney, has a picture ID 'security badge' issued by the Security Division of the Guilford County Courthouse. It enables the writer to use a separate entrance where his 'security badge' is swiped enabling the door to unlock. The Security Badge is issued by each county. It bears the photo of the badge holder together with a badge number, the holder's employment, and an expiration date. Once the expiration date has been reached, the security badge will no longer operate the "swipe" mechanism. The badge can be renewed or reactivated for another year upon payment of a fee and the validation by the Security Office of the card-holder's information. The county keeps a tight control over the issuance and renewal of these Security Badges. Before the above-mentioned cell-phone ban and should a phone ring during a session of court, the owner could be charged with contempt of court and punished by a fine and/or surrender of cell phone. Those who have the privilege of being issued a photo-ID 'security badge' have the obligation of adhering to all of the rules of court so as to preserve the sanctity of court proceedings. Journalists and other people who visit the courthouse frequently can apply to the Office of the Security Director for a pass. The cell phone can be of great convenience to families and friends. However, there is a time and place for everything. Since this convenience can disrupt the importance of the courts' proceedings, appropriate steps have been taken. At this writing, the Rockingham County Courthouse located in Wentworth prohibits cell phones, laptops and other electronics. Randolph and Lee Counties also do not allow any electronics in the courthouse and Rutherford County does not allow cell phones. The gist of this information is to make you aware of these situations as you travel to different counties. You should leave your cell phones and laptops in your cars when you are parked. If any of these electronics contain evidence which need to be introduced at a hearing or trial, you should obtain prior written authorization from either the Trial Court Administrator or the Presiding Judge in that particular county. This written authorization can then be presented to the Security Officers when you arrive at the courthouse. These steps already taken by these particular counties will, in the writer's view, be a precursor for a ban in all courthouses, statewide, of cell phones and other electronics. They will, therefore, fall into the same category of weapons and contraband perceived as a weapons as being strictly banned from all courthouses.

THE CALENDAR CALL

During calendar call, you will often note in large counties that there are attorneys from other counties as well. The length of the calendar will depend on the size of the county and the frequency of court sessions. The smaller the county, the more varied is the type of cases on the calendar such divorces, domestic motions, civil motions and trials, contempt of court causes of action, etc. Larger counties will have calendars dedicated to one type of actions. Often, too, the calendar will include 'clean-up' matters which are either scheduled for hearing or dismissed. It is a good idea to try to have the calendar printed in your office before leaving for court so as to give you "a heads-up" so the time out of the office can be scheduled accordingly.

It is professionally imperative that you stand when addressing the Presiding Judge or when the Presiding Judge addresses you. For gentlemen lawyers, a tie and dark suit is preferred. For women lawyers, a dark pant-suit or other tasteful outfit will suffice. In some smaller counties, some attorneys do remain seated while addressing the Bench and are often addressed by the Judge by their first name. These local customs should not deter you from keeping the proceeding and dress within the formal parameters a court of law demand. Once you have answered the calendar call on behalf of your client, it is suggested that you continue to observe the ebb and flow of the rest of the calendar to determine how your matter will be ultimately positioned for your Hearing or trial, whatever the case may be. You can again review your facts and/ or contact your witnesses, if needed. If you are from another county and your matter should take a small amount of time, the Presiding Judge often will set your case in the early part of the day. This courtesy is granted more times than not.

Seating during calendar call varies from county to county. Often, the jury box is where the local attorneys will congregate. There will be chairs 'behind the bar' on which to seat as well as chairs at the two counsels' tables. It is best to arrive early to assess the seating situation for the calendar call to enable you to blend in with the 'locals'. You will be new to this courtroom and to the bailiff in attendance. When your case is called, you will clearly state your name, the name of your home county and how long feel your case will take to be heard. This, hopefully, will alert the Court of your need to be heard at an early time. Once the calendar is called, the Court will hear matters in the order as set by the Judge.

If your clients have frequent business in this particular county, it is a good idea, before you leave the courthouse, to make it a point to meet the personnel in the clerk's office who process your papers. Your business card should be left with them. Once there is a face to face meeting, future transactions are handled with ease as are the resolutions of any problems should they arise. The court staff have a stressful job and any expressions of gratitude are greatly appreciated.

JUDGES

You are familiar with the Judges who preside over cases in your home county. You know their names and they know yours. You know their mannerisms and temperament. This enables you to prepare for your hearing or trial accordingly. You want to be able to mold your facts with the law in an attempt to obtain a favorable ruling from the Judge or jury as the case may be. When you go to other counties for the first time, you will meet new Judges. You will need to "make a quick read" as to his/her personality and as to how the court is run and how efficiently calendar call and cases are handled. Each Judge and each courtroom is different. You will learn to quickly adapt to the local court mores.

The calendar call itself is addressed in another Chapter. You will be with attorneys primarily from the county in which this court is located. But, expect to be with other attorneys from adjacent counties and often, from beyond. As a rule of thumb, the larger the county, the more other counties will be represented at the calendar call. Some attorneys will travel a hundred + miles. This is made possible by the wonderful highway system available here in North Carolina which is discussed in yet another Chapter. When court is opened on time, it is appreciated by all in attendance. A delay may be occasioned by a 'pre-trial conference in chambers". A pleasantry expressed by the Judge when court is opened seems to set the tone for the morning's activities.

The calling of the calendar and setting matters for Hearing or Trial can be very organized and regimented. This is a must for a large docket and a very large courtroom audience of attorneys, witnesses and family members. The attorneys will be seated in front of "the bar", at attorney tables, surrounding chairs and often in the jury box. You will learn what areas are appropriate for the calendar call. You should arrive early to review your notes and case facts, or perhaps meet opposing counsel to discuss any points of agreements so the court can be so informed when the case is called. Most of the Judges with whom your writer has dealt exhibited the important attributes of courtesy, patience and a keen understanding of the rules of civil procedure and the applicable laws and rules. All of these factors contribute to the ultimate result of fairness for all parties. A Judge must be able to quickly understand and grasp the situation.

In one county, one the of district court Judges was blind. The writer was always amazed as to how this Judge handled each case before him in a competent and judicious manner. He recognized the voices of the local attorneys who appeared before him regularly. Once you introduce yourself to him, your voice, likewise, will be "saved" in his memory. The court proceedings were handled as expeditiously as if the Judge had the sense of sight. The court clerk reviewed all submitted documentation and then placed it in front of this Judge for his signature. The writer will always remember this particular Judge for his courage to proceed in life without the gift of sight. County officials and the local citizenry are to be complimented for giving him an opportunity to do so in this fashion.

One notable Judge wore western boots in Court, a few were rude and short-tempered, another had a wonderful sense of humor, and one could not hear my short motion after a long calendar call stating, "if you only knew how much work I had to do today". It was of no moment that the writer was in court on time and that an eighty mile round trip was involved. This is the risk of handling out-of-county matters. But, all and all, the writer was treated with courtesy and respect, and knowing he was from another county, most would try as best he/she could to hear the Motion that day. In trial situations, the writer would obtain a trial date during that session which would require another trip to this courthouse.

COURT-ORDERED ARBITRATION

When a case is pending in The General Court of Justice, District Court Division in North Carolina, it is subject to be assigned to Arbitration pursuant to NCGS 7A-37.1 and the Rules for Court-Ordered Arbitration. All civil cases involving claims for monetary relief not exceeding $25,000.00 are automatically assigned, with the exception of domestic cases, class actions, special proceedings, d estates, summary ejectments, condemnation actions and more recently, "in which the sole claim is an action on an account". Section 7A-37.1(c) previously made non-binding arbitration optional in civil actions where claims did not exceed fifteen thousand dollars ($15,000.00). + Session Law 2013-159 amends Section 7A-37.1(c) to *require* non-binding arbitration for all civil actions where claims do not exceed twenty-five thousand dollars ($25,000.00), still with the exceptions set forth above.

However, parties have the ability to waive arbitration upon consent of all parties to the action. This 2013 Amendment reflects the increased jurisdictional amount in controversy for the district court division from $ 10,000.00 to $25,000.00.

Section 7A-37.1(c) now not only makes non-binding arbitration mandatory, the increase in the applicable amount in controversy will effectively increase the number of cases required to undergo non-binding arbitration. All parties must be present at the hearing or represented at the hearing by someone authorized to make binding decisions on their behalf in all matters in controversy before the arbitrator who is an experienced trial attorney. The time allocated for the entire hearing is one hour pursuant to Rules of Court Ordered Arbitration, Rule 3 (n). In larger counties, there are courtrooms dedicated to the Arbitration Process. In smaller counties, the arbitration could be heard in a courtroom, if available, in an unoccupied Magistrate's office, in rooms formerly used by the local Sheriff, an unoccupied grand jury room or any other public room in the Courthouse suitable for conducting judicial proceedings. Annex courthouse buildings are also often used for this purpose. The Annex could be connected to the Courthouse or in a separate building as part of the Courthouse Complex, as the case may be. This is an opportunity to exchange information which supports the claims of the parties in a pre-trial setting.

Many matters have been settled either during or after the arbitration hearing. In any event, the award by the Arbitrator is non-binding and an aggrieved party can request a trial *de novo* within thirty days of the award, paying the required costs into the court. If there is not a request for a trial *de novo* within the thirty day rejection period, the award of the arbitrator will be adopted by the Court as its Judgment, which is non appealable. Rule 3(b) of The Court-Ordered Arbitration in North Carolina requires a pre-hearing Exchange of Information at least (10) days before the date set for hearing. Failure to provide all parties with any documents (10) days prior to the hearing is a ground for its exclusion at the hearing. All copies of exchanged documents or exhibits are admissible in Arbitration Hearings under Rule 3(d). It is important to complete your Pre-Arbitration Submission of Information.

The writer often prepared a "Plaintiff's Brief in Arbitration" which included Statement of Facts, Law & Argument and Conclusion to be tendered to the Arbitrator and opposing parties or counsel at the Arbitration Hearing. A copy of the Pre-Arbitration Submission previously prepared and served upon the opposing party or opposing counsel would be attached to the Brief together with supporting exhibits would be tendered to the Arbitrator when the our client's case was called for argument. This evidence should be carefully prepared before travelling to the out of county Arbitration Hearing and reviewed before the actual Hearing. Once at the County Courthouse, allot additional time to find the place for the Arbitration should it not be in a designated courtroom. After the Arbitration Hearing, each party is obligated to pay a statutory fee. Those who are unable to pay can have the payment waived upon the signing an affidavit of financial impairment. A copy of the Arbitrator's decision is either given to, or mailed to, each of the parties. This procedure lifts the weight of any qualifying case from a congested court docket. Accordingly, this type of Alternative Dispute Resolution has served its purpose. You have travelled to the county in question and have represented your client in the fashion as ordered by the Clerk of Court. Future Arbitration Hearings in this county, or any other, can now be handled more confidently.

NORTH CAROLINA HIGHWAY HISTORICAL MARKERS

A bonus to traveling out of county to attend court is the opportunity to learn more about the history of our State from North Carolina Highway Historical Markers also known as "history on a stick" or "history by the spoonful". These markers are under the supervision of the North Carolina Department of Cultural Resources. In 1935, the North Carolina General Assembly established a program to "provide for the erection of markers at points of historic interest along the public highways". To be eligible for a state marker, a subject must be judged to be of statewide historical significance. These markers are placed only on state or federally numbered highways but cannot be located on interstates or limited access routes. Each county in North Carolina has a number of Highway Historical Markers which commemorate the significant happenings locally.

The writer passes a number of these Markers each day. A prominent Marker in downtown Greensboro concerns the "SIT-INS' which 'launched the national drive for integrated lunch counters. Feb 1, 1960 in Woolworth store 2 blocks south'. The 'Woolworth store' in question is now the International Civil Rights Center and Museum. Another concerns "O.HENRY" in the person of William Sydney Porter, 1862-1910, short story writer, lived in a house which stood 'near here'. The writer's law office is said to be on or next door to the location of this house. On the corner of Wendover Ave. and Church St. here in Greensboro, a marker commemorates "CONE BROTHERS" and states that "Moses and Ceasar Cone pioneered marketing of textiles; manufactured denim & flannel. Their first mill, Proximity, 1895, was 1/4 mile N.E". In the process, Cone Mills became one of the world's largest producers of denim, flannel and corduroy. The city of Greensboro and the state of North Carolina continue to benefit from the foresight and generosity of the Cone family.

One day after court in Rowan County, the writer happened upon a Marker near the courthouse captioned "WASHINGTON'S SOUTHERN TOUR". It states that President Washington was a visitor in the town of Salisbury, May30-31,

1791. This lead the writer to learn more about this 'southern tour', when it began and when it ended. It was learned that this 'southern tour' at that time was heading north and that the next and last stop was 'GUILFORD COURTHOUSE' in Greensboro. Its Historical Marker is located at the intersection of Battleground Ave and New Garden Road and states: 'Important battle of the Revolution between armies of Greene and Cornwallis. U. S. military park'. This battle took place on March 15, 1781. This battle was not only the largest, most hotly-contested battle of Revolutionary War's Southern Campaign, but is considered pivotal to the ultimate American victory. Although the British force under the command of Lt. General Charles Cornwallis defeated the American force under the command of Major General Nathanael Greene, the British army sustained such heavy casualties that the result was a strategic victory for the American force and merely a *Pyrrhic Victory* for the British forces. Several months later, the British forces surrendered in Yorktown to Major General George Washington. In essence, the first President of the United States, as he was leaving North Carolina, was paying homage to this sacred battle site ten years later.

On April 28, 2014, a State Highway Historical Marker relating to the HIGH POINT MARKET was installed on

South Main Street near the historical furniture exposition hall. The first formal Southern Furniture Market was held in High Point in March, 1909. The Southern Furniture Exposition Building opened on June 20, 1921 having 249,000 square feet of exhibition space. In 1989, the Southern Furniture Market was renamed the International Home Furnishings Market. The Market currently has 10.5 million feet of showroom space, 180 buildings, roughly 2,000 exhibitors and approximately 75,000 attendees each Market which is held in April and in October each year. This Market is considered the largest home furnishings industry trade show in the world.

This is just a small example how these wonderful Historical Markers can invigorate and produce the desire to learn more about the historical happenings in North Carolina. As stated above, these Historical Markers are located in every county and can be enjoyed on your way to and fro the court house. Although the Markers are not on Interstate Highways, they are prevalent in and around the city or town which serves as the county seat. During a lunch time break, a stroll through town is often relaxing and educational should you encounter Historical Markers. You learn about the county and county-seat in ways not before known. All counties have their own personalities, influenced by local industries and/or businesses. You will find Historical Markers commemorating the establishment of schools, colleges, hospitals, roads, meeting places and churches, the birthplace of famous persons, the site of the establishment of companies and enterprises which became known nationally and, often, world-wide and the location of events which changed the course of history. Each of North Carolina's three geographic regions has its own distinctive history, natural scenery and recreational opportunities. At this writing, there are in excess of 1,500 sites in North Carolina where history happened. The sites are commemorated by an official state highway Historical Marker.

On November 1, 2016, the Greensboro Medical Society unveiled an HISTORICAL MARKER commemorating the decision by the Fourth Circuit Court of Appeals in *Simkins v Moses H. Cone Memorial Hospital*, 323 F. 2nd 959 (4th Cir. 1963). The opinion effectively desegregated hospitals nationally by holding that the "separate but equal" standard was unconstitutional as applied to publicly funded hospitals. This marker is located on the east side of North Elm Street adjacent to Moses H. Cone Memorial Hospital.

In 1962, six physicians, including Dr. Alvin Blount, three dentists and two patients filed suit against Moses H. Cone Hospital and Wesley Long Hospital. When that suit was resolved in 1963, the effect was felt across our Nation. African-American physicians secured the right to practice medicine at previously segregated hospitals and African-American patients were allowed admission to hospitals under the same terms and conditions as white patients.

In this Federal suit, the Plaintiffs found a legal loophole through the federal Hill-Burton Act which said Federal dollars could not be used to discriminate. The 4th Circuit Court of Appeals agreed. This case was considered as important to integrating hospitals as Brown v Board of Education was to integrating schools.

Dr. Blount was the first African-American doctor to operate at Moses H. Cone Memorial Hospital. He died on January 6, 2017 at the age of 94. He will always be remembered as "one of the men who opened Moses Cone to everyone."

NORTH CAROLINA WILDFLOWER PROGRAM

Another bonus found as you travel North Carolina highways to attend court in other counties is beautiful wildflower beds along North Carolina's interstates and U. S. Highways, often as far as the eye can see. The North Carolina Department of Transportation Wildflower Program began in 1985 as an integral part of highway beautification. Proceeds from the sale of personalized license plates and donations fund this $1.3 million annual wildflower program. Wildflower beds are installed and maintained across the state in each of the fourteen highway divisions. These beds at this time are strategically located on approximately 1,500 acres of roadside land. The vibrant colors often temper and soften a mood which may have been affected by your court proceeding and the results attained.

Seas of red, yellow, white, orange and pink have the capacity to stimulate your emotions and are often a welcome relief from the monotonous chore of driving distances from your home. You will find the white Ox-Eye Daisy as well as the dashing Red Corn Poppy, also known as the Flanders Poppy or Shirley Poppy. The vibrant orange belongs to the California Poppy. The brilliant pink belongs to Catchfly also known as Sweet William Catchfly. The eye-catching yellow is that of the popular Lance-Leaved Coreopsis. Combinations of white, pink and red are provided by the Corn Poppy. Bicolor of yellow and red, pink, white or purple are produced by Toadflax, also known as Baby Snapdragon. The eastern part of the state features Lance leaf Coreopsis, Red Corn Poppy and Pink Catchfly. Central North Carolina favors the Ox-Eye Daisy, Lance leaf Coreopsis, California Poppy as well as Sweet William Catchfly. Ox-Eye Daisy is prevalent in the western part of the state together with Red Corn Poppy.

Soil types and average temperatures are part of the deciding factors as to which wildflower will flourish along the roadsides in the different parts of the state. The months of April through August are the months of color. The Fall will have color from the turning of the leaves, The Winter boasts bright and colorful reflections from the icy dew and of course, the Spring welcomes new growth heralded by the yellow Forsythia. In North Carolina, you will enjoy color the year-around. It is important you embrace and appreciate these colors and works of nature, all of which will make your travels to the various courthouses more pleasant and mood-lifting.

The wildflower gardens along our state's interstates and highways were the brainchild of former North Carolina First Lady Dottie Martin. The Texas Wildflower Program was her inspiration. Former First Lady Ladybird Johnson spearheaded the beautification of highways and the planting of flowers in Texas. Here in North Carolina, the hundreds of wildflower beds along the roadsides are installed and maintained by the Roadside Environmental Unit of the North Carolina Department of Transportation. The DOT asks motorists, by appropriate signage, not to stop and pick the wildflowers. First of all, it is not safe and secondly, it is important to leave them for all to enjoy.

The wildflower program is a year-long effort. After the soil is prepared, the beds are fumigated to eliminate competition from weeds and grasses until the wildflowers are well established. For best results, seeds are sown from September through November or from March through May. The beds are mulched with either coastal Bermuda hay, pine straw or fine pine bark. Unless there is an extended dry period, the wildflowers once planted will require little or no maintenance. Carolina lily (*Lilium michauxii*) is the official state wildflower as designated by the North Carolina General Assembly in 2003 (NCGS 145-20). This perennial flower grows throughout the state, from Cherokee County with its forests and hills to Hyde and Pamlico Counties with their coastal habitat. Although not now utilized in the state's roadside wildflower beds, it is sure to be a prized possession of gardeners and private landowners. This nodding flower's petals are brilliant red-orange and with brown spots. It has an arched back with the tips overlapping near the top of the stem. It is an elegant flower but even in *mass plantings*, it would not produce the "wow" factor as do the yellows, reds, whites, etc. when driving along the interstates and state highways.

While on vacation, many enjoy looking at and identifying wildflowers down country roads where they can safely walk. There is an abundance of wildflower books for every part of the country. In every region, many flowers have only local distribution. Often, some flowers can be fairly common in a range of just a few counties. It is good to remember that the leaves and stems, rather than the blossoms themselves, are diagnostic for field identification. Accordingly, one should concentrate on the green parts to match against the ID in a wildflower field guide. One should also be careful not to trespass on private property.

Wildflower beds are installed and maintained throughout the state by workers with the North Carolina Department of Transportation Roadside Environmental Unit in each of the highway divisions. Awards are given to the best-looking flower beds in each region as well as the best over-all highway division wildflower program. The North Carolina Transportation Secretary has said: "From improving the environment to encouraging economic development and tourism, the Wildflower Program not only makes our roadways more attractive, but it also contributes to North Carolina's over-all quality of life".

<u>CONCLUSION</u>

I hope you will find my observations beneficial as you practice law in the State of North Carolina, which practice often entails having to travel to another County on behalf of your client. This necessity, from time to time, removes you from the comfort of your home-county surroundings and from the familiar faces of local court personnel and fellow attorneys. My observations were gleaned from years of travel to other North Carolina Counties. As I noted, and as will be noted by you as well, changes are constantly underway whether it is a new Courthouse, the disappearance of a familiar parking lot, the closing of a convenient coffee shop or the new highway configurations to meet the standards of the growing Interstate and State roads systems. Changes are the natural process for growth and progress. You will be making your own mental notes of these changes in each of the Counties you will visit. The rigidity of the law that you practice, however, will withstand the wind of any environmental changes. Before you undertake any journey to another county, it is important that you thoroughly prepare your case. Once you arrive at your destination, you will be engaged, otherwise, in finding the courthouse, finding appropriate parking and finding your courtroom. In one of the previous chapters, I did suggest, if you wished, the use of pre-recorded information containing your facts and argument. This would make good use of your hours at you travelled. It was a pleasure for me to share my experiences in this tutorial of my observances along the way. It is hoped that all travels are made safely and with confidence. And that successful results will follow, as well. If anyone benefits from this tutorial, it has served its purpose for now and in the future.

Robert M. Weinstein, Esq.

Printed in the United States
By Bookmasters